Power in Times of Uncertainty

Training Your Mind
To Change Your Life

Julie Petrella, Ph.D.

ISBN 0-7414-2140-2

Cover design by Tom Graney
Photography by Tom Graney

Published by:

INFI∞ITY
PUBLISHING.COM

1094 New Dehaven Street, Suite 100
West Conshohocken, PA 19428-2713
Info@buybooksontheweb.com
www.buybooksontheweb.com
Toll-free (877) BUY BOOK
Local Phone (610) 941-9999
Fax (610) 941-9959

Printed in the United States of America

Printed on Recycled Paper

Published July 2004

Dedication

This work is dedicated to my parents (both the earthly and the heavenly) - your abundant unconditional love awes me fantastically and inspires me to live boldly in pursuit of my dreams.

Acknowledgments

I would like to extend my gratitude to the following people who made the completion of this book possible:

To my family – Mom, Pop, Marcus, Tammy, Gianna, Luca, Grandma, and Grandpa (who is missed, but not forgotten) – thank you so much for all of your love and support and also for reminding me that all things are possible. Special thanks to Mom, who has been my guide and my coach through everything. (Mom, you are my guru.)

To my beloved, Eric – thank you so much for being with me through this, and for just being you. I am so thankful for the peace and joy you bring into my life.

To my friends - Amy, Donna, Karen, Lisa, Teresa, and Tina – you are my extended family. Thank you so much for being my sisters and my confidants.

To Tom Graney, thank you for creating a beautiful cover through your creativity and artistry.

To my editor, David Breidenbach, thank you for your expertise and meticulous work. You were a tremendous help.

Thanks again, I love you all!

Contents

On Writing this Book: A Letter to the Reader

Dear Reader,

When I'm looking for answers I want them to be simple, straightforward, and to the point. I've dedicated the last 12 years of my life to human learning and performance, and I've found that even the most complex human functioning can be made simple enough for everyone to understand. So I followed the K.I.S.S. rule and made this book simple. There's no jargon and no fifty-cent words in this book.

I also value your time. This book contains information that I've gleaned through my professional experiences and education, and also from reviewing the literature on psychology, philosophy, and systems science. Although the information sources are wide and varied, I know you don't want to waste hours sifting through fluff and filler just to find the main points.

Years ago when I worked for the Army, a wise Sergeant friend of mine once said, "Don't give 'em a toolbox when all they need is a wrench." So, dear reader, here is your wrench. Use it in good health.

Abundant blessings,

Dr. Julie Petrella

Overview

"The greatest discovery of my generation is that man can alter his life simply by altering his attitude of mind."
William James

Who hasn't had times of uncertainty? We are constantly faced with uncertainty in our work, our personal lives, and our family lives. The uncertain situations could be of a large magnitude, such as ending a relationship, starting a new career, or moving to a new city. They could be on a smaller scale, but still have a high impact, like giving a presentation, waiting for that important phone call, or having a disagreement with a family member.

An uncertain situation can be on our minds constantly, like "How am I going to pay the bills?" It could be a fleeting thought, like "What was *that* supposed to mean?"

Beginnings or endings, good news or bad news, situations in which the outcome is unknown will always present themselves.

Uncertainty is inevitable. How we handle uncertainty affects the level of success we achieve in life. When uncertain times arise, some people will stand strong while others are knocked down.

Consider the example of two trees in a storm. Picture a bright and sunny afternoon on a perfect summer day. Seemingly out of nowhere a thunderstorm hits. The wind begins to howl, and the two trees rock back and forth. After hours of rain, lightning, and wind, one tree falls to the ground. The other tree, which took as much of a beating from the storm as the fallen tree, still stands and appears untouched. One tree could withstand the harshest environment and the other could not.

Like the trees in the storm, some people will remain standing in the face of uncertainty while others collapse from environmental influences. Some people will have happy and healthy relationships, peace of mind, and a sense of control in uncertain times. Others will have strained relationships, feelings of helplessness, and a lack of self-control when times are uncertain. The question is, why are some people able to withstand uncertain times while others are not? How can some people seem to be comfortable in even the most uncomfortable circumstances? Is it luck? Is it genetic? The simple answer is that it all begins within your mind.

Powerless and Powerful Modes

Although each person faces unique life situations, we will all operate in one of two "mind modes" when uncertain times arise. Strained relationships, feelings of anxiety, and thoughts of helplessness are all marks of a person who is operating in what I call the *Powerless Mode*. This is the mode in which the mind tells us to feel powerless in times of uncertainty.

In the Powerless Mode, we feel like we are just waiting for the storm to be over, just hoping to survive. In this mode, we think that *the environment has total control of our lives.* We give all of our power away. When we are in the Powerless Mode, we may experience some of the following thoughts or feelings listed below.

❑   We think that we are victims of circumstance.

❑   We think that we are puppets on a string, controlled by our boss, our spouse, our family, our friends, or society in general.

❑   We think that we have no control.

❑   We think that we have no choices.

❑   We think that we are alone.

As a result of being in the Powerless Mode, we will often:

❑   become destructive to others

❑   become destructive to ourselves

❑   wallow in self-pity or "poor me" thinking

❑   avoid important issues or problems

❑   blame others for our own mistakes or shortcomings

❑   point out everything that is wrong with other people

❑   put out a phony image of ourselves to the world

❑   generate or fall to addictions

Chances are, you will be able to think of quite a few people who have exhibited these types of behaviors. They are not difficult to spot. If you are willing to go a step further, you will be able to think of times in your own life when you have exhibited behaviors of the Powerless Mode. Let's face it, we've all been there, done that, got the T-shirt.

Luckily, there is an alternative to the Powerless Mode. You guessed it – it's called the *Powerful Mode*. In the Powerful Mode, the mind tells us to feel powerful in times of uncertainty. In the Powerful Mode, we view uncertainty as a challenge to conquer rather than a hardship to endure. In the Powerful Mode, we can face the storm, because we know that we control the way we think about, and what we do about, our life situations. We know that *the environment affects us, but it does not control us.* In the Powerful Mode, we also know:

❏   We are not victims.

❏   We have control.

❏   We make our own choices.

❏   We interact with our environment by what we think and do.

❏   We have options.

As a result of being in the Powerful Mode, we will:

❏   have confidence and trust in ourselves

❏   have appreciation for others

❏   have the perseverance to keep going

❏   confront tough issues or problems

❏   take personal accountability for our words and actions

❏   have self-discipline and balance in our lives

❏   live with personal integrity and values

Often times people confuse being in the Powerful Mode with having authority. Having authority means that you can make decisions that affect people or events in your immediate environment.

If you are a teacher, you have authority over your classroom. If you are a manager, you have authority over your employees. Feeling powerful has nothing to do with having authority. Feeling powerful has everything to do with controlling your own thoughts and your own life. Feeling powerful is knowing that you can weather and outlast all of the personal storms that you will face in life. Remember that you can feel powerful with absolutely no authority. Conversely, you can feel powerless with loads of authority.

The Cause

Knowing that there are two modes, why would we choose to feel powerless? Why would anyone choose to go through the pain and the fear of feeling out of control? Why would anyone want to treat others badly? Why can't we just say we want the Powerful Mode and then flip a switch? Asking these questions would be like asking the question, "Why does it rain?"

In ancient times (and in modern times in some places), people would do a rain dance when they wanted it to rain. When it finally rained, the people thought that the dance *caused* the rain. But now in modern times, we know that the rain dance really did not *cause* the rain. In ancient times, people had a very limited perspective when it came to rain. Now, we have the tools that give us a "bird's eye view" of rain. There is an entire process of evaporation, condensation, and precipitation that is constantly at work that actually causes the rain. Although a person cannot see, touch, or hear most of the process, it is still there, causing the rain day after day, year after year. The process is timeless and universal.

So it is with the Powerless and Powerful modes. Like the rain, there is an underlying process that actually *causes* us to feel powerless or powerful in times of uncertainty. Although uncertain situations differ among people, the Powerless and Powerful modes are timeless and universal. Whether you are a salesperson, a teacher, a lawyer, a scientist, a stay-at-home parent, a student, or a soldier, you will operate in one of these two modes when uncertain times arise.

Also, like the rain, the process that causes the Powerless and Powerful Modes is not easily observed. You can't see it, you can't hear it, and you can't touch it. For this reason, most people do not even know that a process exists. In this book, you will discover this process. Then, you will have the tools that give you a "bird's eye view" of the thought processes that directly affect your life.

Training Your Mind

Knowing what causes us to feel powerless or powerful in times of uncertainty is key because once you find the cause, you can find the solution.

Consider the example of cold medicine. It gives you temporary relief from symptoms of a cold. It does not prevent you from getting a cold again. Now, consider a vaccine. A vaccine ensures that you will not get sick again from the same virus. Why? A scientist develops a vaccine by figuring out how the virus works, namely what *causes* the virus to attack the body, and then they develop the solution.

Unlike the process that causes rain*, **we can control the Powerless and Powerful modes.*** It all begins with your thoughts – nothing more. For thousands of years, we have known that our thoughts create our words and actions, which in turn, create our lives. Marcus Aurelius, a Roman Emperor who ruled around 161 AD wrote, "A man's life is what his thoughts make it." That seems like common sense, right? Watch an interview with any athlete and they will say that their sport (regardless of which one it is) is mostly a mental game. That is, they win because of what is going on in their own minds. Such is life. The problem is that, like most things, it's easier said than done. Even though we know that our thoughts create our lives, we don't take the time to figure it out. Instead, we often end up defeating ourselves. We don't take the time to train our minds.

Think of this book as a vaccine for your mind. This book will give you insight into what *causes* you to be powerful or powerless when uncertain times arise. Once you have gained the insight, you can then learn to **train your mind** to be powerful in times of uncertainty. When you train your mind to be in the Powerful Mode, you'll have more confidence, better relationships, and more control of your life. You'll learn to be comfortable in even the most uncomfortable situations. You'll realize that your environment affects you but does not control you. Once you train your mind, you'll change your life.

Recognizing the Powerless Mode

"Being powerful is like being a lady. If you have to tell people you are, you aren't."
Margaret Thatcher

Now I'm assuming that you don't want to continue with this mode, but I've included it because knowing what *not to do* is more than half the battle. The great military leader, Sun Tzu, wrote the following passage in his famous work, ***The Art of War:***

Knowing the other and knowing oneself,

In one hundred battles no danger.

Not knowing the other and knowing oneself,

One victory for one loss.

Not knowing the other and not knowing oneself,

In every battle certain defeat.

In essence, the concept here is that in order to win the battle, you must know "the other" (the Powerless mode) as well as "oneself" (the Powerful mode). This chapter is about knowing "the other." Knowing everything you can about the Powerless Mode will help you defend against it when you feel yourself slipping in that direction.

The Powerless Mode at a Glance

The process of the Powerless Mode occurs in your mind. The Powerless Mode is not a constant or steady state. We can be in the Powerless Mode for a few minutes a day, for a few days at a time, or for years on end. If we were to look at the Powerless Mode in the form of a still picture, it would look like the following diagram.

The Powerless Mode

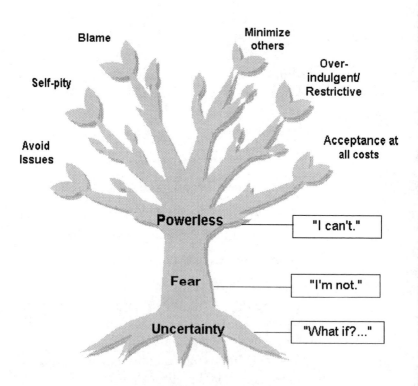

This is the tree that gets toppled when a storm of uncertainty comes. The tree gets knocked down because the roots are not strong enough to hold it. Like weak roots in a tree, uncertainty is the root of the Powerless Mode. Like a tree, each element in the Powerless Mode feeds and builds upon the other. Also like a tree, all of the parts of the Powerless Mode are different, but together the parts make up the whole.

Uncertainty: The Root of the Powerless Mode

The root of the Powerless Mode begins when a person focuses on uncertainty. An uncertain situation, event, or thought occurs, and the person immediately starts a barrage of "What if?" questions. The "What if?" questions usually deal with one of three categories: general, rejection, or betrayal. Listed below are some examples.

General

- ❑ What if this doesn't work out?
- ❑ What if this is a wrong decision?
- ❑ What if this is just a pipe dream?
- ❑ What if this wasn't meant to be?
- ❑ What if this is a dumb idea?

Rejection

- ❑ What if they don't like/love me?
- ❑ What if they don't think I'm good enough?
- ❑ What if they leave me?
- ❑ What if they fire me?
- ❑ What if they don't hire me?
- ❑ What if they don't have confidence in me?
- ❑ What if they don't take me seriously?
- ❑ What if they think I'm a failure?
- ❑ What if they don't forgive me?

Betrayal

- ❑ What if they lie to me?
- ❑ What if they cheat on me?
- ❑ What if they make fun of me?
- ❑ What if they say bad things about me?
- ❑ What if they turn their back on me?

When a people place their focus on the uncertainty of their own environment, the "What if?" questions go on and on. The fact is, everything is going to change at some point. (Wouldn't life be boring if it was the same all of the time?)

The root of the Powerless Mode is focusing on *what we don't want to happen*. The funny thing about "What if?" questions is that they are typically things that are beyond our control anyway. For example, you could be the perfect husband/wife, but that doesn't guarantee that your spouse won't leave. You could be the best employee, but it doesn't mean that your ideas will always be valued. You could be the nicest person in the world, but it doesn't mean that people won't say ugly things about you behind your back.

When we spend too much time and energy on "What if?" questions, we will most certainly internalize the "What if?" into a feeling – and that feeling is fear.

Fear: The Trunk of the Powerless Mode

The next level in the Powerless Mode is the feeling of fear. I'm not referring to healthy fear, such as fear of heights, deep water, or wild animals. I'm also not referring to the Stephen King kind of fear or the fear of haunted houses. The fear I'm referring to is much more insidious. It is the fear of "I'm not." The "I'm not" is typically used in relation to "I'm not enough."

- ❑ I'm not good enough.
- ❑ I'm not worthy enough.
- ❑ I'm not strong enough.
- ❑ I'm not smart enough.
- ❑ I'm not experienced enough.
- ❑ I'm not articulate enough.
- ❑ I'm not attractive enough.
- ❑ I'm not able to deal with this.
- ❑ I'm not as good as so and so.

Translation: I'm not sure of myself. Why do you think that the number one fear among people is public speaking? I mean, public speaking ranks above heights, closed-in spaces, everything! It is a perfect example of an "I'm not" fear.

The terrible thing about the fear of "I'm not" is that it makes a person forget all of the good things they are. A person forgets how good, how strong, how smart, and how worthy they are in exchange for fearing what they are not. That doesn't sound like a good tradeoff, does it? As a result, rather than looking at what *can* be done, the person looks at what *can't* be done, and thus begins to feel powerless.

The Branches of the Powerless Mode

The branches of the Powerless Mode, are well - feeling powerless. Because the person is focusing on what *can't* be done, they feel out of control. Some examples of "I can't" include:

- ❑ I can't handle this.
- ❑ I can't get out of this situation.
- ❑ I can't start over again.
- ❑ I can't get over this.
- ❑ I can't deal with anything else.
- ❑ I can't get control over this.
- ❑ I can't try something different.
- ❑ I can't make a difference.

There is nothing left to do, no choices, no options, no power. The person stops contributing and stops connecting with others. The mindset dictates that they sit on the sidelines and just watch others do great things, since they have no power. They let things happen, and never make things happen.

Typically, when a person is in a mindset of feeling powerless, they will execute at least one (if not all) of these approaches:

1. Give up and just concede to feeling powerless.

2. Become destructive to others so that they will feel more powerful.

3. Become destructive to themselves so that they feel a sense of power. (I know this sounds crazy, but it's true!)

The Leaves/Fruit of the Powerless Mode: A Profile of Characteristics

This is where we see the results (or fruit) of thinking in the Powerless Mode. The results manifest as our attitudes and behaviors, namely, the way we treat others as well as ourselves. There are probably hundreds (maybe even thousands) of attitudes and behaviors that can surface in the Powerless Mode, but I've listed a few of the most common and easily recognizable.

Avoid issues

One characteristic of the Powerless Mode is when people avoid the important issue at hand. They may deny that there is an issue. (What problem? Things couldn't be better! My life is just perfect!) Because the person avoids issues, they usually avoid people or situations that will challenge them to confront it. They become defensive when expected to confront the issue, and thus project their emotions onto other people. (What are you talking about? You're crazy! You're jealous! You don't know what you're talking about! I don't want to talk about it!)

Someone who avoids issues is not only irritating to others, but is also destructive to themselves. Did you know that if your mind is experiencing a stressful situation, then your body will have responses to it no matter how hard you try to avoid it or forget about it? Stress can change your heart rate and blood pressure. Prolonged periods of these changes can result in many physical ailments: impaired immune function, headaches, sleep disorders, and abdominal pain just to name a few. So, even if a person avoids the issue on the surface, the stress still affects the body.

Self-pity

This characteristic is fairly easy to spot. It is marked by "poor me," "why me," "nobody cares," and "it's not fair." A person in self-pity typically complains about what a hard life they've had, how they have nothing, and how much everyone else has. (You can almost hear the violins in the background...) A person in self-pity has a sense of entitlement in that they feel that the things they want in life are a birthright, instead of something requiring their time and effort to get. This is the "the world owes me a living" mentality. In essence, this person thinks, I can't hack it, so *you* have to take care of it for me. At worst, a person wallowing in self-pity becomes an emotional vampire. They suck the energy and resources out of everyone around them, since they refuse to work for anything on their own.

Blame

"Passing the buck." We've all heard of it, and we've all done it. When people feel powerless, they often attribute blame to others when they can't think of a good enough reason as to why they did or didn't do something. There is no accountability for their own actions. Every hardship is due to someone or something else. (Interestingly enough, they normally attribute every good thing to themselves!)

When this person wants something and can't have it, it's *your* fault. When this person wants to do something, but doesn't do it, it's *your* fault. When this person is unhappy, it's *your* fault. The finger is pointed everywhere except for the mirror. This person has an excuse for everything and accountability for nothing.

Minimize Others

Comedian George Carlin once jokingly said, "If you can't beat 'em, arrange to have 'em beaten". That just about sums it up. In the rules of logic, there is a fallacy called ad hominem. When a person can't think of a logical retort to an argument, they attack the person they're arguing with instead. An example is a person saying something like, "I'm not going to discuss this anymore, because you are nothing but a _____ anyway." Put any kind of label in the blank – bastard, bitch, conservative, liberal, chauvinist, man-hater, whatever. Minimizing others implies name-calling. A person who feels powerless will seek to take any feeling of power away from others to give themselves a sense of power.

There are countless ways in which people minimize others. Basically, people who minimize others think that everyone else is too old, too young, too fat, too thin, etc. They may minimize a person's knowledge or experience. (You don't understand. What could you know? You don't know anything about X.) They may minimize a person's education or job. (You mean you *didn't* go to college? You work *at that place*?) Worst yet, they may minimize a person's appearance. (Look at that suit, it's awful. Who does she think she is wearing that outfit?)

Over-indulgent/Over-restrictive

I listed these two together, because both indicate a lack of self-discipline. When a person feels powerless, they often seek to gain power by what they take in or keep out of their bodies. As a result, this creates a "high" or feeling of power. Over-indulgent behavior can turn into addictions of all kinds - drugs, alcohol, sex, food. On the other end of the spectrum, there are disorders that involve over-restriction, such as anorexia nervosa or bulimia.

Over-indulgence and over-restriction are also not limited to physical aspects. A person can over-indulge in daydreams or fantasies as well. I'm not referring to momentary daydreams about your next vacation, dream job, or ideal partner. What I'm referring to is a state in which the person is so engulfed in their fantasy world, that they start giving more energy to their fantasy world than they give to their reality. This gives the person an illusionary sense of power and an imaginary escape from feeling powerless. The unfortunate thing is that the person eventually has to come back to reality, and when they do, they will probably have more problems to solve than what they started with.

Acceptance at all costs

Because the person is feeling powerless, they do not believe that they are worthy in and of themselves. Thus, they begin to seek acceptance from others at all costs. Think of a gang. Gangs are groups of people who do stupid (and typically criminal) things for no other reason than to belong to the group.

Next, think of the "fake," the "phony," the "sell-out". This is the person who will do anything to belong. Whether it's owning the "right" car, having the "right" house, wearing the "right" clothes, hanging out with the "right" people, or putting their child in the "right" pre-school. The truth is, this person has no idea what "right" is because they have to ask everyone else.

The Powerless Mode within You

The key to overcoming the Powerless Mode is to recognize how it operates within you. When we review the previous paragraphs about how to recognize the Powerless Mode, it may be easy to see in others, but much harder to recognize within yourself. Even though the characteristics of the Powerless Mode are described in the third person, the fact is that the Powerless Mode lives in all of us.

Oftentimes, we get so busy with life that we simply don't slow down and observe our own thoughts or behaviors. We do not take the time to figure out why we say or do certain things. Also, we tend to compare ourselves to others, and as a result we put ourselves in one category and our mates or co-workers into another. The point of learning about the Powerless Mode is to understand how it works within *you*. It is not about others. You can only control you.

To find areas in your life where you may be feeling powerless, start at the top of the tree model (the leaves/fruit), and ask yourself when you have exhibited any of the characteristics that are listed. Then, work your way down the tree, asking yourself what led you to think or behave in those ways. Use the Self-Reflection questions listed below to help you uncover uncertainty in your own life situations.

Self-Reflection

1. Look at the profile of characteristics in the Powerless Mode. Can you think of a situation in which you exhibited at least one of these?

2. In this situation, in what way did you feel out of control? What was your "I can't"?

3. Keeping in mind the way you felt out of control, what were you really afraid of? What was your "I'm not"?

4. What were you really uncertain of? What were your "What ifs"?

Recognizing the Powerful Mode

"In the midst of winter, I found there was within me, an invincible summer."

Albert Camus

The Powerful Mode allows us to look at uncertain times through a different lens. We don't have to slip into fear and a powerless mindset. When you looked at the Powerless Mode, the concept was "knowing the other." In this chapter, the overarching concept is "knowing oneself." In the Powerful Mode, we know that the outside environment cannot affect our sense of self, and therefore, this is the mode in which we truly know ourselves. Knowing how to immediately recognize characteristics of the Powerful Mode will guide you back if you find yourself getting lost and heading toward the Powerless Mode.

The Powerful Mode at a Glance

Like the process of the Powerful Mode, the process of the Powerful Mode also occurs in your mind. You can't see it, hear, it or touch it, but nevertheless it is there. Like the Powerless Mode, the Powerful Mode is not a static state. We can be in the Powerful Mode temporarily or for most of our lives. If we look at the Powerful Mode in the form of a still picture, it would look like the following diagram.

The Powerful Mode

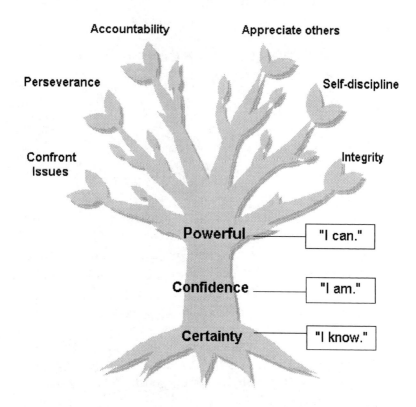

This is the tree that withstands the storm. The tree stays intact because of its strong roots. The Powerful Mode is the antithesis of the Powerless Mode. Where there was uncertainty, there is certainty. Where there was fear, there is confidence. Where there was no power, there is power.

Certainty: The Root of the Powerful Mode

When an uncertain event, situation, or thought occurs, rather than begin to focus on the "What if?" questions, people in the Powerful Mode focus on the "I know." Regardless of whether the uncertainty deals with general feelings, rejection, or betrayal, people in the Powerful Mode answer feelings of uncertainty with "I know."

General

- ❑ I know that no matter what, I will be OK.
- ❑ I know that things will work out for the best.
- ❑ I know that things happen for a reason.
- ❑ I know that I'm here for a reason.
- ❑ I know that there is something greater than myself.

Rejection

- ❑ I know that I'm worthy.
- ❑ I know that I'm good enough.
- ❑ I know that I will find someone else.
- ❑ I know that I will find another job.
- ❑ I know that I have unique gifts and talents.
- ❑ I know that I make sound decisions.
- ❑ I know that I've done my best.
- ❑ I know that I will do better next time.
- ❑ I know that I have good intentions.

Betrayal

- ❑ I know that I can trust my instincts.
- ❑ I know that I will get through this.
- ❑ I know that I am loved.
- ❑ I know that I am watched over.

❑   I know that I am not alone.

When people focus their minds on certainty, they think about what they **want to happen**. Unlike uncertainty, in which people focus on what they cannot control, people with certainty (a) focus on what they can control, or (b) give up what they cannot control to a higher power. (It is interesting to note that on studies of resiliency, the common factor among people who could thrive in the worst of conditions was a belief in a higher power.)

People with certainty focus on their knowledge, their experience, and their belief system. They do not waste time busying their minds with things beyond their control. Rather than spinning their wheels with all the "What if?" questions, they ground themselves in what they inherently know. Oprah Winfrey has a great monthly column in her *O* magazine. It's called "What I know for sure." A person in the Powerful Mode would surely have a long list.

Focusing on the "I know" results in a sense of confidence.

Confidence: The Trunk of the Powerful Mode

The next level in the Powerful Mode is the feeling of confidence. Confidence entails a feeling of self-esteem and self-trust. These people know that they are w orthy and they trust in their ability to make decisions. It is also a feeling of knowing that they can do what they set out to do. As opposed to the fear of "I'm not," this is the "I am."

❑   I am good.

❑   I am strong.

❑   I am smart.

❑   I am knowledgeable.

❑   I am resourceful.

- ❑ I am attractive.
- ❑ I am able to make sound decisions.
- ❑ I am able to deal with this.
- ❑ I am a unique individual.
- ❑ I am worthy.

No matter what the world tries to tell this person, regardless of labels that may be assigned, this person does not bother with what they're *not*. They have an innate sense of who they *are*. For example, the boxing champion Muhammad Ali, used to say, "I am the greatest." Not only did he know it, but so did others. He was named "Athlete of the Century" by Sports Illustrated and USA Today. (Imagine Ali saying, "I'm not as good as the other guy." Sounds strange, doesn't it?)

There is, however, a paradoxical quality to being confident. A person has to earn confidence by first experiencing fear. Sound strange? Theoretically, confidence would not exist without fear. The fact is, if a person has not been fearful at some point, then they cannot truly know what it is to be confident. This is called the law of opposites. On a more practical level, if a person hasn't been knocked down, then they haven't experienced getting up and starting again. It is the getting up and starting again that gives a person confidence. It gives a person the "I am." The authentic "I am" leads to a mindset of "I can."

The Branches of the Powerful Mode

The feeling of power in the Powerful Mode is based in the "I can." This person knows that they can contribute their knowledge and talents in a meaningful way. Listed below are some examples of "I can."

- ❑ I can handle this.

❑   I can get out of this situation.

❑   I can start over again.

❑   I can get over this.

❑   I can deal with this.

❑   I can get control over this.

❑   I can try something different.

❑   I can make a difference.

Because the mindset is "I can," this person also knows that "no man is an island." They know they need resources. As a result, they connect with others and build strong support systems. Within their support systems, they tend to be strong "givers," but they also know when to ask for help. This person is not the spectator, but the one in the arena, sweating it out, knowing that they make things happen. This person knows that there are always options. If there does not seem to be a way, then they will either *find* a way or *make* a way.

Typically, when a person's mindset is one of feeling powerful, they will use at least one (if not all) of these approaches:

1.   Face issues head on.

2.   Be appreciative of and gracious to others.

3.   Have high expectations of themselves.

The Leaves/Fruit of the Powerful Mode: A Profile of Characteristics

As in the Powerless Mode, people will manifest certain attitudes and behaviors, or characteristics, as a result of feeling powerful. Listed below are some of the most commonly recognizable characteristics of people in the Powerful Mode.

Confronts issues

These people are the ones who grab the proverbial bull by the horns. Rather than sit around and complain about how things are, they confront the issue head on. They are problem-solvers and want to be part of the solution. This is not an easy task. Most of the time, it is easier to just let things be, to just let it ride, to just hope it will go away. Most of us have been in situations where it was scary to confront the truth. Even though it would be easier just to avoid the issue altogether and hope that it will go away, these people willingly step outside their comfort zone to meet the challenge.

These people confront issues because they know that they will either pay now or pay later. Just like dealing with credit card debt, they know that it's easier to just handle it now, because issues, like debt, tend to build up over time. These people travel light, because they are not weighed down with lots of old baggage from the past. It has already been handled.

Perseverance

When I think of perseverance, the first thing that stands out in my mind is my first trip to Italy. I remember talking to a young guy who told me that it was a good thing to approach as many women as possible. He said, "This way, you may get slapped by ten women in one day, but the eleventh one may say yes." This is a humorous example, of course, but it does capture the spirit of perseverance.

These are the people who do not give up, no matter what. Regardless of what the world tells them, they don't allow themselves to entertain the thought that they will end up in failure. The world's greatest minds have made testimonials to perseverance.

"I haven't failed, I just found 10,000 ways that don't work."

Thomas Edison

"I think and think for months and years. Ninety-nine times, the conclusion is false. The hundredth time I am right."

Albert Einstein

"...and still, I rise."

Maya Angelou

Accountability

This is the opposite of blame. People with accountability understand that it is up to them to make choices. They decide what to say, how to react, with whom they associate, what they read, what they eat, where they go, and how they handle their situations from this point on. They are completely accountable for their own actions.

These people take credit where credit is due – good or bad. They do not blame others for their mistakes, and they do not expect others to lead their lives for them. These people are very wise, because they know what they don't know. Instead of indulging in the fantasy that they are perfect and that they know everything, they realize that they are fallible, and they search for knowledge and new ways to approach their lives. If they hurt someone's feelings, then they apologize and make sure that it doesn't happen again. No blaming, no excuses, no pity party. End of story.

Appreciate Others

Unlike people in the Powerless Mode who minimize others, these people know how valuable others are. They do not have to wait until it's gone to know what they have. This person knows that no one can make it alone, and maximizes on the wisdom and support that others give. They are not afraid to show their gratitude, because they are coming from a mindset of power. Not only does this person give genuine compliments to people in their lives, but they are also helpful and supportive in return. They know how to give, and they also know how to receive.

These people have a true appreciation for others because they can empathize with them. Rather than look at others as being different and separate from them, they can understand others shortcomings, because they are aware of their own. Because this person is coming from a mindset of power, they can also show appreciation for others' gifts without envy. They do not feel as if they are losing something by lifting others up. Instead, they enjoy doing so. This person is happy when others thrive.

Self-discipline

People in Powerful Mode know that they may have to experience some discomfort in achieving what they want. Self-discipline is about doing what needs to be done in order to achieve a goal. Remember the movie, *Rocky?* Rocky, the boxer, got up before the sun came up, ate raw eggs, and ran through the bitter cold streets of Philadelphia. (I can hear the theme song in my mind....)These people do not have time for excuses, and take charge of their own minds and bodies when it's time to get the job done. Unlike the person who over-indulges, this person can say "no" to things that are destructive to their mind or body. Maybe this person would rather lay on the couch and watch an old movie, but instead they get up and exercise. Because the person is coming from a mindset of "I can," they have the will and the spunk to override the short-term in order to create better things for the long-term.

Also, people who have self-discipline know when they need to rest, take a break, or just do something else. They do not over-indulge, but they do not over-restrict either. They know that having some fun today will help them relax so that they can be more productive tomorrow. Just because they are willing to experience some discomfort, it does not mean that they shut out comfort altogether. They take care of themselves, and are kind to themselves.

Integrity

You can take what these people tell you to the bank, because they will stick to their ethics and values regardless of what others say. Unlike people who seek acceptance at all costs, people with integrity are willing to do the right thing even if it makes them unpopular. Although these people are loyal, they do not allow their loyalty to outweigh their integrity, and are therefore willing to say no to others when necessary. Listed below is my favorite quote on integrity, and I think that she said it best.

> *"Do what you feel in your heart to be right – for you'll be criticized anyway. You'll be damned if you do, and damned if you don't."*

> *Eleanor Roosevelt*

The Powerful Mode within You

Like the Powerless mode, the Powerful mode may be easy to recognize in others, but much harder to recognize within yourself. We often compare ourselves to others may not see the Powerful Mode within. As mentioned in the previous chapter, the Powerful Mode, like the Powerless Mode, resides in *all of us*. When you find your own keys to certainty, then you can begin to train your mind to be powerful regardless of your situation. Use the Self-Reflection questions listed below to uncover where to find certainty in your own life situations.

Self-Reflection

1. Look at the profile of characteristics in the Powerful Mode. Think of a situation in which you exhibited at least one of these.

2. In this situation, in what way did you feel in control? What was your "I can"?

3. Keeping in mind the way you felt in control, what were you confident about? What was your "I am"?

4. What were you really certain of? What were your "I knows"?

Training Your Mind to Be in the Powerful Mode

"I am, indeed, a king, because I know how to rule myself."

Pietro Aretino

Training the mind is just like training the body. Athletes perform an exercise regimen to train their bodies in order to achieve the results they want. With more training, one's body gets stronger. Professional athletes have to train several hours a day, but recreational athletes may only train a few hours a week. The amount of training depends on your desired end result. So, the amount of training you put in for your mind is going to depend on the results you want. Do you want to be powerful in all situations or just some of them? Do you want to be powerful today or for the rest of the year? In this chapter, I will provide a training regimen for your mind.

After you've read this chapter, use the Power 10 Worksheet and examples included in the back of the book to help get you into the Powerful Mode.

The Training Regimen

Now that you are aware of the processes that cause the two mind modes, you are ready for the training regimen.

When an uncertain event, situation, or thought arises:

1. Neutralize the uncertainty within your mind.

2. Focus your energy on certainty.

3. Anchor yourself in the Powerful Mode.

4. Set boundaries.

1. Neutralize the uncertainty within your mind.

The most effective way to deflect the Powerless Mode is to cut it off at the root. The way to do this is to neutralize uncertainty by answering those pesky "What if?" questions with "I know" responses. Use the self-reflection exercises in Chapters 1 and 2 to aid in doing this. For example:

If your question was:	Answer it with:
What if this doesn't work out?	I know that I will be OK no matter what.
What if they don't think I'm good enough?	I know that I have unique talents and skills.
What if they don't take me seriously?	I know that I've done my best.
What if he/she leaves me?	I know that I will find someone else who appreciates me.
What if I can't find another job?	I know that I have skills, knowledge, and talent, and that someone is looking for these things specifically.

These are just a few examples, but regardless of your situation, I'll bet that you can find at least one strong "I know" for every "What if." The fact is, your "What if?" questions will continue to play in the background of your mind like a song until you fully answer the question.

A tricky aspect to answering your "What if?" questions is realizing that they exist. There are two common reasons for this difficulty. The first is that often, we don't even want to admit that we have them. We want to be strong and confident, and we don't want to face our own feelings of uncertainty. We want others to think of us as confident and powerful, and sometimes we don't like to admit uncertainty and fear because we don't want to look like we're not in control. The second reason is that we may get into a situation that is so overwhelming, so fast, or so tense, that we spend too much time reacting to the situation to become aware of the "What if?" questions.

If by chance you find difficulty in figuring out your specific "What if?", then use the military strategy of "taking the high ground." In ancient times when soldiers fought hand-to-hand, they were busy reacting to the clubs and swords coming at them. They could not see anything other than what was in front of them at the time. Good military leaders would take a higher ground (a hill, for example) and look down at the battle to assess the situation. When the leaders looked down at a battle, versus staying in it, they gained a big picture point of view, and were able to develop tactics to defeat their opponent. This was one of the advantages of taking higher ground. (Another, of course, was to force their opponents to fight uphill!)

So, when you find yourself reacting to the uncertain things being thrown at you, first, take a higher ground in your mind. Step out of the "battle" so that you can make a better assessment of what is going on. Act as if your are an observer of the situation, and not actually taking part in it.

Imagine that you would have to give advice to someone else in your situation. This will give you a wider and broader perspective.

2.   Focus your energy on certainty.

OK, now that you've neutralized your uncertainty, the next step is to focus on certainty. It sounds easy enough. But, we as human beings are so interesting. We will continue to focus on the "What ifs" (what we don't want) instead of the "I know" (what we do want).

Years ago, I took a class on motorcycle riding. One of the first things I learned is that you have to look where you want to go. Your body, and thus your motorcycle, will go in whatever direction you look. So, if you want to turn left, look left. One of the biggest mistakes a beginner can make is to focus on an obstacle. For example, let's say that I'm learning to ride and a car pulls out in front of me. My tendency is going to be to look at the car, because I don't want to hit it. But, if I focus on the car, then that's exactly where my motorcycle and I are going to go. I have to look in the direction I want to go (away from the car) in order to avoid a crash. This is exactly the point for focusing on certainty.

Research consistently shows that when people are faced with an uncertain situation, they will focus more on potential losses than potential gains. Thus, our natural tendency is to focus on what we *don't* want, instead of what we *do* want. If you focus on what you want, or if you focus on what you don't want, inevitably, that's exactly what you'll get.

Returning to the example of motorcycle riding, you'll either get away safely or you'll crash. That is why it is so important to focus completely on certainty. If you find the "What if" questions replaying over and over in your mind. Simply say "stop." Redirect your focus on your "I know," and don't even for a minute look the other direction. Babe Ruth, arguably one of the greatest baseball players of all time, is credited with stepping up to the plate and pointing to where he was going to hit the ball before the pitch. This is a beautiful example of focusing energy on certainty.

3. Anchor yourself in the Powerful Mode.

Think about what an anchor does for a boat. It keeps the boat from floating away. It keeps the boat where the captain wants it to be. If you want to be in the Powerful Mode, and not veer over into the Powerless, you must use some anchors of your own.

The anchors you can use are your "I am" and "I can" statements. (For examples of "I am" and "I can" statements, see Chapter 2.)Think of a time in which you felt extremely powerful. What "I am" and "I can" thoughts were going through your mind? Make a list of these. Being aware of your own "I am" and "I can" will show you exactly how you made the journey through the Powerful Mode before, and therefore will serve as an anchor for you again. Secondly, knowing your specific "I am" and "I can" will help you understand your boundaries and how to set them, which is step #4 in the formula for getting into the Powerful Mode.

4. Set boundaries.

The first three steps explain how to get into the Powerful Mode. The last step is about staying there. Sometimes events, situations, or thoughts will attempt to breach your mindset of power. To keep this from happening, you must set boundaries. What do I mean by boundaries?

Picture a medieval town. Around this town is a huge wall. Past the wall is a deep moat filled with water. The town has the wall and the moat to protect from intruders. However, the town from the inside is open to the sky. The townspeople need light and heat from the sun, and they need rain water. So, they try to keep out what may hurt them and let in things they need. These are boundaries. You need to be able to construct your own boundaries to protect yourself from things that may try to knock you out of the Powerful Mode. In addition, you need to be sure that you are letting in the things that will keep you there.

For example, if you know that certain people in your life are always trying to pull you down and keep you in the Powerless Mode, then you must distance yourself from them and block out their influence. This does not mean, however, that you should isolate yourself from the world. It means that you should find other people who support you in the Powerful Mode. The key is to shut out bad influences and let in good ones. This applies to people, things, and thoughts in your own mind. Take a look at the list below and ask yourself whether you are keeping these things out or whether you are letting them in.

Keeping out or Letting in?

❑   People who take every opportunity to remind me of what I'm *not.*

❑   People who support me and remind me of what I am.

❑   Thoughts of "I can't."

❑   Thoughts of "I can."

❑   People who tear others down to make themselves feel better.

❑   People who show appreciation for others.

❑   Books, movies, or TV shows that depress me.

❑   Books, movies, or TV shows that inspire me.

❑   Music that makes me want to cry.

❑ Music that makes me want to sing or dance.

❑ Doubts about my abilities.

❑ Opportunities for success.

In addition to the items above, compile your own list of things that you keep out or let in on a regular basis.

Things I Keep Out	Things I Let In

Do these things support a mindset of being powerful or do they support a mindset of being powerless? Do you think that these things are supporting the "I know," the "I am," and the "I can" within you, or do they incite you ask more "What if?" questions? This will facilitate your discovery of what boundaries you need personally to keep you in the mode of power.

Once you have discovered the boundaries you need to create or adjust, make a conscious effort to stick to them. This may require that you change your habits, redefine your relationships, or change your thought patterns. It may seem like quite a bit of work, but if you put the effort in now, then the results will be well worth it. Best of all, you won't have to hang around feeling powerless.

In addition to what we keep out and let in, another aspect of boundaries is what we let go of and what we hang on to.

Remember the Kenny Rogers song, *The Gambler*? Depending on where you live and how old you are, you may or may not, but there is a line in the song that goes, "Every gambler knows the secret to surviving is knowing what to throw away and knowing what to keep." Like a good card player, a person who wants to stay in the Powerful Mode needs to know what to hang on to and what to let go of.

Take a look at the categories below, and then perform an inventory of the things that you are hanging on to and the things that you have let go of.

Hanging on or Letting Go?

- The past
  - Events
  - Relationships
  - Conversations
  - Lifestyle
- The future
  - Dreams
  - Pursuits
  - Hopes
  - Goals
- Labels that have been assigned to you
- A hobby or interest that you're passionate about
- A job, relationship, or lifestyle that no longer suits you

Things I Hang On To	Things I Let Go Of

Once you've performed your inventory, you can add anything else that jumps out in your mind with regard to letting go or hanging on. Then, ask yourself why you are hanging on to or letting go of these things. Are these things supporting the "I know," the "I am," and the "I can" within you, or do they incite you to ask more "What if?" questions? Do you feel powerful when you hang on to or let go of these things? Make a conscious decision to let go of things that incite a powerless mindset within you, and hang on to the things that support a powerful mindset.

I know, it's easier said than done. People write entire books and develop very specific therapeutic programs with the desired goal of letting go. Like I said in the beginning, the objective of this book is to give you a wrench and not a whole toolbox. In order to let go of something that has been very influential in your life, you may need more than just a wrench. If this is the case, you may need to seek counsel from a professional who specializes in this type of process.

Tips for Setting Boundaries

In addition to the difficulty of letting go, there are other challenges with regard to setting boundaries. Whether it's about keeping out, letting in, hanging on, or letting go, time and time again we all go through challenges when we set new boundaries. Any change will always bring challenge. Listed below are some tips that can help you overcome some common obstacles you may run into when setting boundaries.

1.   Do not let others steer you off course.

Basically when you set boundaries, you want to do something that is different from what you normally do. It could be that you want to stop hanging out with gossipy friends so that you can meet friends that are kinder and more supportive. It could be that you ask to be treated differently than the way someone is used to treating you. It could be that you want to take that opportunity for a more fulfilling, but lesser paying job. It could be that you just want to think about things from a different perspective. You've set your new boundaries, and you have a renewed sense of certainty. Then, when you go looking for support, you suddenly find yourself all alone.

People may not like your new boundaries. They may say, "What's wrong with you? You never seemed to care about this before. Why now? What are you trying to prove?" The fact is, when you begin to set new boundaries, it may scare others around you because it may imply that they have to create new ways of relating to you – new ways of treating you, new ways of supporting you, new ways of thinking about you. If they think that there is something wrong with what you're trying to do, then so be it.   Stick to your boundaries, and above all, do not feel guilty about it. The good news is that if you stay with your new boundaries, then others will eventually re-learn how to treat you and think about you.

2. Set boundaries one at a time.

Sometimes when we want to set a boundary, it just seems like such a big change. Setting the new boundary looks so big, and requires so many changes at once, that we think it will be nearly impossible to do it. For most of us, it is difficult to take on a boundary that implies many changes all at once. Take for example, a person who wants to break away from "friends" who like to criticize and gossip in search of friends who are kind and supportive. They've associated with these "friends" for years, and now they want it to stop, but it just seems impossible. It affects so many things - weekends, vacations, holidays, mutual acquaintances. There are so many things that have to change, and the person just feels overwhelmed, like it's too much.

The key here is to set boundaries one step at a time. Meaning, do one small thing. Next, do something that requires a little more effort. Work your way up to setting more difficult boundaries by practicing with easier ones. For example, the person who wants new friends could start by limiting their time spent talking with their old friends. They could start a new hobby or join a new organization without the old friends. They could start spending more time with new friends, until finally, they simply break away from the old friends. This way, the smaller boundaries build up to the big one. In this case, the end boundary is eventually set, but with much less impact since it was done one step at a time.

3. Don't get too comfortable.

We've all heard of the comfort zone. We all have a comfort zone. For all of us, it can be difficult to get out of. Even if we don't like the way things are, it's what we know, so it's what we're comfortable with. When you think about setting a boundary, it may seem easier not to do it, because setting a new boundary requires work on your part. Of course it seems easier to just hang around and feel like you have no control.

It seems easier to blame others. It seems easier to make yourself feel better by putting others down. However, just because it seems easier does not mean that it is better. We know for sure that these things will not lead to power.

A wise man once told me that when you're faced with a decision in which you have two options, the more difficult one is usually the right one. Such is true with setting boundaries. It may seem harder to do, but our greatest gains in life tend to arise from difficulty. Think about it, what have you really gained from something that was easy? *Besides, are you going to exchange power for easy?*

A final note on boundaries...

Staying in the Powerful Mode requires that you protect your position with boundaries. When setting boundaries remember to:

♦ Keep out thoughts of "What if," "I'm not," and "I can't."

♦ Let in thoughts of "I know," "I am," and "I can".

From there, the key to setting boundaries is to stack the deck in your favor. Set boundaries that are likely to keep you in the mindset of feeling powerful. What you keep, let in, hang on to, or let go of is up to you. Build your walls, but also remember to let the sun shine in.

Appendix A

Summary of Principles

Summary of Principles

❏   When faced with times of uncertainty, we operate in
    one of two modes – Powerless Mode or Powerful
    Mode.

❏   In the Powerless Mode:

> 1. We think that we are victims of circumstance.
>
> 2. We think that we are puppets on a string,
>   controlled by our boss, our spouse, our
>   family, our friends, or society in general.
>
> 3. We think that we have no control.
>
> 4. We think that we have no choices.
>
> 5. We think that we are alone.

❏   In the Powerful Mode:

> 1. We are not victims.
>
> 2. We have control.
>
> 3. We are in charge of our choices.
>
> 4. We create our environment by what we think
>   and do.
>
> 5. We have options.

❑ The Powerless Mode at a glance looks like this:

The Powerless Mode

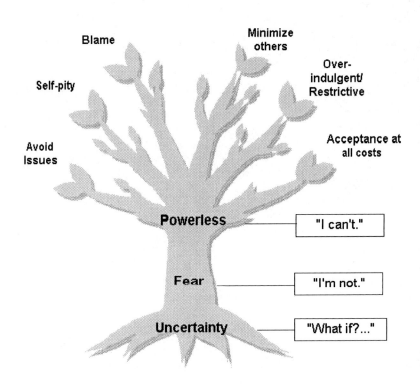

❑   The Powerful Mode at a glance looks like this:

The Powerful Mode

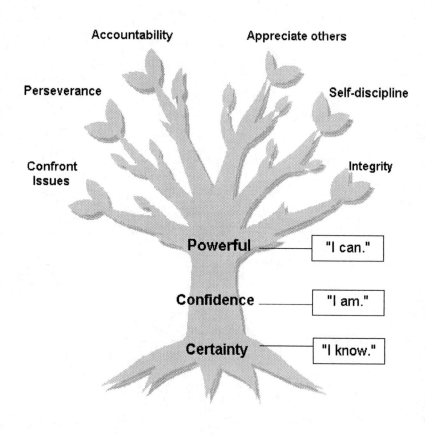

❑ To train your mind to be in the Powerful Mode:

1. Know the Powerless and the Powerful modes.

    This is knowing the cause, effects, and characteristics of each mode.

2. Neutralize the uncertainty within your mind.

    Answer your "what if?" questions with "I know."

3. Focus on certainty.

    Focus on where you want to go. Don't focus on where you don't want to be, or what you don't want to happen.

4. Anchor yourself in the Powerful Mode.

    Become aware of your unique "I am" and "I can" statements.

5. Set boundaries.

    Protect your mindset of power by knowing what helps you and knowing what hurts you. Decide what you need to keep out, let in, let go of, or hang on to. Follow through with new, stronger boundaries.

Appendix B

Power 10 Worksheet

Power 10 Worksheet

Purpose: This worksheet will guide you through the process of training your mind to get into the Powerful Mode when faced with uncertainty. The worksheet covers the main principles presented in the book in just 10 questions.

Using this worksheet: It's simple. Just follow the directions and fill in the blanks. If you have trouble clarifying your responses, take a look at the examples in Appendix B.

Questions

1. What is your uncertain situation? Describe this situation in detail. (If you can't think of a situation specifically, but just have a generalized feeling of not being in control, go to question #2.)

2. Look at the profile of characteristics in the Powerless Mode (Chapter 2). Describe how you are exhibiting any of these.

3. In this situation, in what way do you feel out of control? What is your "I can't"?

4. Keeping in mind the way you feel out of control, what are you really afraid of? What was your "I'm not"?

5. What are you really uncertain of? What are your "What ifs"?

6. Answer your "What ifs" with "I know".

7. Focus on certainty. Then, make a list of your "I am" and a list of your "I can".

8. Look at your current boundaries with regard to your situation. What are you keeping out, letting in, hanging on to, letting go of?

9. Focusing on your "I know," "I am," and "I can," adjust your current boundaries or set a new boundary.

10. Look at the profile of characteristics in the Powerful Mode (Chapter 3). Describe which Powerful Mode characteristics you will replace for your Powerless Mode characteristics.

Appendix C

Power 10 Worksheet Examples

Power 10 Worksheet Examples

To provide some real-life examples of how the Power Worksheet can help you, I conducted some interviews with some folks using this worksheet. They generously shared their own real-life situations with me. Under the stipulation of keeping their names anonymous, I included two of the worksheets as examples for you to use. I hope that their responses will guide you in finding your own answers.

Example #1 – Marital Problems

Questions

1. What is your uncertain situation? Describe this situation in detail. (If you can't think of a situation specifically, but just have a generalized feeling of not being in control, go to question #2.)

   I am having marital problems. Our relationship is on the brink of falling apart. I think that either he is going to leave or that I am going to leave. We just don't seem to connect anymore. We are polite to each other, but that's about it. I feel like I'm living with a roommate instead of a partner. I'm completely miserable.

2. Look at the profile of characteristics in the Powerless Mode. Describe how you are exhibiting any of these.

   *I **blame** him for everything. He just doesn't seem to understand me or what my needs are. I feel like he doesn't care. I am probably in denial about the fact that I am somehow contributing to all of this. Even though I* *don't want to live this way, I don't feel like dealing with him, so I'm **avoiding the issue**. I don't want to lose him completely, but I don't know if we can make it work. I do feel like I **minimize** him in a lot of ways.*

3. In this situation, in what way do you feel out of control? What is your "I can't"?

   I can't live like this. I can't handle leaving him, either.

4. Keeping in mind the way you felt out of control, what are you really afraid of? What is your "I'm not"?

   I'm not attractive enough. I'm not interesting enough. I'm not fun. I'm not worth it.

5. What are you uncertain of? What are your "What ifs"?

   What if we really do split up? What if we can't fix this? What if we make a huge mistake?

6. Answer your "What ifs" with "I know."

   I know that I will survive. I know that I am strong. I know that if we put our minds to it, then we can fix this. I know that I've made some mistakes in the past, and I've learned from them. I know that I won't make the same mistakes again.

7. Focus on certainty. Then, make a list of your "I am" and list of your "I can."

   I am caring. I am level-headed. I am a good person. I am worthy of love. I am a kind person.

   I can face this. I can talk to him. I can come up with other options. I can try my best.

8. Look at your current boundaries with regard to your situation. What are you keeping out, letting in, hanging on to, letting go of?

   I realize that I was trying to let go of my responsibility in this, and that I need to hang on to it. I'm hanging onto what our relationship used to be, how good it was. In a lot of ways, I've been keeping him out, too. I should make an effort to let him in, to talk to him more. I'm trying to hang on to the reason I married him.

9. Focusing on your "I know," "I am," and "I can," adjust your current boundaries or set a new boundary.

   I can focus on now, instead of the past.

   I know why I married him.

   I can let him into my life more than I have been.

   I can find options other than leaving him.

   I can accept responsibility for my part in this.

10. Look at the profile of characteristics in the Powerful Mode. Describe which Powerful Mode characteristics you will replace for your Powerless Mode characteristics.

> *Accountability – I will be more accountable for my own actions*
>
> *Appreciate others – I will appreciate the good things in our marriage*

Example #2 – Career Fears

Questions

1. What is your uncertain situation? Describe this situation in detail. (If you can't think of a situation specifically, but just have a generalized feeling of not being in control, go to question #2.)

   No matter how hard I try to please her, my manager just doesn't seem to like me. Any time I ask her a question, she doesn't have time to answer it, but later she yells at me and tells me that I did something wrong. She is a really moody person, and I can't seem to figure her out. I know that I haven't done anything wrong, so I don't know why she is so mean to me. I feel like she could fire me at any point, which would probably be a relief, but I don't want to get fired. So, maybe I'll just resign. But, I'm afraid that she will give me a bad reference. I'm not sure what to do.

2. Look at the profile of characteristics in the Powerless Mode. Describe how you are exhibiting any of these.

   *I have a lot of anxiety about this whole thing. Sometimes I find it hard to sleep at night, and one day I went home crying. Now that I think about it, I do try to get her to **accept me** by doing things that I normally wouldn't do. Like, I laugh when she makes rude comments about other people. I just go along with it. I have also **lost weight** during the last couple of months because I'm too stressed out to think about* *eating right now. Instead of eating dinner, I've been having a few glasses of wine every night just so I can sleep.*

3. In this situation, in what way do you feel out of control? What is your "I can't"?

   I can't deal with this. I can't convince her of anything. No matter what I do, I can't change this situation. I can't keep doing this.

4. Keeping in mind the way you felt out of control, what are you really afraid of? What is your "I'm not"?

   I'm not likeable. I'm not strong enough to confront her. I'm not smart enough. I'm not doing something right.

5. What are you really uncertain of? What are your "What ifs"?

   What if I ask her why she is so mean to me, and then she yells at me again? What if I quit and then she gets mad? What if I can't find another job? What if she gives me a bad reference, and then nobody else will hire me? What if she can control my future?

6. Answer your "What ifs" with "I know."

    I know that I can handle it, because I've handled it before. I know that I haven't done anything wrong. I know that I will find another job. I know that I am a good worker, and I know that a bad reference would be a lie. I know that she cannot control my future. I know that I have more control over my life than she does. I know that other people would love to have me on their staff. I know that she is just one person.

7. Focus on certainty. Then, make a list of your "I am" and list of your "I can."

    I am a good worker. I am a likeable person. I am smart. I am qualified. I am a nice person.

    I can do this. I can leave this job and this boss. I can start looking for another job now.

8. Look at your current boundaries with regard to your situation. What are you keeping out, letting in, hanging on to, letting go of?

    I've been keeping out the opportunity for a better job with a better manager. I'm hanging on to her criticisms. I'm hanging on to thinking that she may be right about me. I'm hanging on to a situation that is not good for me. I am hanging on to anger.

9. Focusing on your "I know," "I am," and "I can," adjust your current boundaries or set a new boundary.

   I can find another job.

   I know that I can start looking immediately.

   I can let go of her criticisms, and not take them to heart.

   I can let go of thinking that she is right about me.

   I can let go of this job and the negative feelings about this experience.

   I can use my anger to motivate myself to make a change.

10. Look at the profile of characteristics in the Powerful Mode. Describe which Powerful Mode characteristics you will replace for your Powerless Mode characteristics.

    Confront issues – I will confront this issue, and stop trying to avoid the fact that I need to find another job.

    Integrity – I will show integrity by not allowing her or anyone else to treat me this way again.